LEGENDS OF DOE HOE

Poems by Jameson Bayles

Kansas City   Missouri

Spartan Press
Kansas City, Missouri
spartanpresskc.com

Copyright (c) Jameson Bayles 2017
First Edition 1 3 5 7 9 10 8 6 4 2
ISBN: 978-1-946642-03-5
LCC#: 2017931035

Design, edits and layout: Jason Ryberg
Author photo: Joan Koromante
Cover photo: Jon Bidwell
All rights reserved. No part of this publication may be reproduced or transmitted in any form or by any means, electronic or mechanical, including photocopying, recording or by info retrieval system, without prior written permission from the author.

ACKNOWLEDGMENTS

Prospero's Books and Spartan Press would like to thank
Jeanette Powers, J. D. Tulloch, Jason Preu, M. Scott
Douglass, Shawn Pavey, Shaun Savings, Jesse Kates,
Jim Holroyd, Steven H.Bridgens, Thomas Mason,
Beth Dille, Mason Wolf, Katherine Samet, The West Plaza
Tomato Co. and The Robert J. Deuser Foundation
For Libertarian Studies.

Special thanks to Jason Ryberg, Mark Hennessy,
John Dorsey, John Burroughs, Dianne Borsenik,
Juliet Cook, Richard Robert Hansen, Christian O'Keeffe,
Dave Church, Charles and Tiffany Cooper, the Kingsley
family, the Bayles family, Mike the bus driver of the 142
in KCMO, and a very special thanks to the Dorie Renee
Hogan Family.

Some of these poems have appeared in *2016 Hessler Street Poetry Anthology* (Crisis Chronicles Press), *Delirious* (Night Ballet Press), *A Case For Ascension* (Asinimali Publications), *The Cataman Years* (Mistop Publications), *The Artistic Muses* (True Colors Press), *Your One Phone Call, Thirteen Myna Birds, Thorny Locust, Open Mic at the Bean, Poems – For-All,* and *Rusty Truck*

CONTENTS

an open letter to the legends of doe hoe (a prelude to suicide which is cheaper than you would think) / 1

the nature vs nurture overdose / 6

sibling rivalry / 9

an open letter to Ronald Johnson / 10

hollow swallow / 13

the hangover of Topeka only lasts until the bottle is empty downtown / 14

click clack paddy whack the Baron needs a home / 16

the engagement / 19

present day / 20

entry number nineteen / 22

her thursdays / 24

the winter of my discontent / 26

the five breaths / 28

an open letter to Lew Welch written by an answer to a question no one asked / 33 an open letter from three plenty of fishes / 37

preface / 39

murphy's law / 41

self help / 42

searching for a voice / 43

the acoustical resonance when doves cry / 45

until the last tie is broken / 46

the biography of Christian O'Keeffe / 48

rides in / 49

one last chance
Is all I get
one last change
Is all I need

given is two,
give me one

one more chance
to prove myself

one chance
out of three

Excerpt from *tecumseh whispers*
by Dorie Renee Hogan
Poems For All #1515

an open letter to the legends of doe hoe
(a prelude to a suicide that is cheaper than
you would think)

dear Dorie,

this antiquated gunshot
started off as a
bloodstained note,
an emancipation proclamation
a sexton of the Tecumseh Cemetery
branded as a Robert Frost rip-off...

*Many woods are dark and deep but as you well
know, the sea of seen is finite...the sea of unseen is
infinite. This collection
of work would not have been conceived
without you ... it would not have been produced without
you...it would not have been reciprocated without you.
Interred in discoutenance,
I glance inside the isles of hypermnesia and
this text glares back with a vengeance. My
motivation was "shasei"...to penetrate
into the true aspect of
reality/nonreality and sketch
life that is a union of nature and of the self.*

*this was your gift to me...
this work is my gift to you…*

abbreviated pauses slumber in between
the invariable spaces entranced among
random snow encased tombstones displayed
during the hangover of nightmares
some would define
as anamnesis

you transcended reality
on a disingenuous
highway cascaded among
amputated footprints Dorie

October 22, 1996

in retaliation,
my suicide today will be a
human vestige among
the emaciated field of
recoiled regret
some would
ascertain as
enlightenment

eleven minutes, it takes
eleven minutes for me to delve into six
inches of snow to exhume the
borders of your tombstone. mirrored
memories drip from the
ruptured messages that I have
baptized and aborted at your grave

*There were 55 of them Dorie....fifty five...I can't
remember all of their names*

Dorie,
in the realm of social encounters,
you were the only territorial sage that mattered
every other woman
who outvied my life

were vacationers
on expired travel visas
pilgrimaging
into the void
of redundancy

stumbling out of the Tecumseh Cemetery,
my eyes become a divorced mist of tears

the tsunami of memory begins

*Dorie wouldn't have felt anything at the moment
of impact....i just want to be friends...a mile east of
Big Springs...did you get the poem that i
mailed you...after her 1992 Mercury Topaz collided
with a
western bound semi heading to Montgomery
Ward, a Lawrence bound sedan
flew 200 feet
before landing in the
embankment...blunt force head trauma...closed
casket funeral... I just want you to trust me...*

I've been
gargling Beretta misfires
Dorie
6:45,
6:55,
7:05 am

a manuscript of fallen angels
slumbering in sleet
hand in hand with
bloodied halos and blue
innuendos evict me out of Kansas

the sexton has also asked me to leave

closing time

yet the rumors remain

the legends of doe hoe evaporating into
every thought I've claimed as my own

> *doe hoe sewed a homemade veil into*
> *her prom dress…doe hoe scattered random*
> *poems among the tea leaves*
> *of youth…doe hoe would want you to move*
> *on from the accident…I just want you to trust me*

this open letter
is a prelude
to a suicide
that is cheaper
than you would think

> *There were 55 of them Dorie....fifty five...I can't
> remember all of their names*

Sincerely,

Jameson Bayles

the nature vs nurture overdose

I watched my years
stain the stationary from
a Holiday Inn condemned
in the afterbirth of Topeka, KS

It was 1975

Vietnamization was out, an
evolution of domestication
was in

Jim rechristened me
      fatherless
that afternoon

retired Army dog tags, *the collected
works of western thought* and
30 silver dollars minted during
the Nixon administration were
impeached to a shoebox

      jimmie lee

inscribed within the tobacco
stains on the lid

I haven't worn Adidas since

Mother absconds a blank father's
day card and
three broken crayons,
from the motel lobby

> *write something for daddy*

dignity
has a
death
all its own

I wrapped Jim's dog tags around my throat
the noose of growing pains
conscripted the ascension of dissension
of my toddler rebuttal

> *Regurgitating the film of*
> *regret and the stench of*
> *You*
> *was adultery*
> *self-preservation*
> *or sel(flesh)?*

> *You never*
> *could fillet*
> *very well,*
> *father*

Mother casts the $30 into the motel register
for another day's rent as I slept on the
mantra of Machiavelli and William James

Dad's dog tags
encamped
around my throat

He was AB negative,
of which I am positive
during my nature vs nurture overdose

sibling rivalry

*If I flunk
all of my classes
this year,
I will still pass.*

*I'm having the teacher's baby
and
I'm going to be
the principal's grandfather.*

> *Fine,
> but clean your room
> before you go.*

an open letter to Ronald Johnson

Dear Mr. Johnson,

tornado alley helps Dorothy keep
Toto's amber waves of grain enslavement on a leash

barebacked by Brownback,
a hollowed coffee cup has been barking
back at me for a week and a half

a buck fifty in change and four
atta boys are all I could harvest today

I don't know Dorothy

when I was three, father told me
that the first four rows of corn
in any field were
by the people, for the people

> *Graduation time,*
> *It's live and let live out here son*

a 30 ought six dissented

resting comfortably in STP stained overalls,
VC shrapnel interred in his left shoulder,
Farmer Love Bones was one hell of a shot
father walked with a limp for a week
I haven't seen him since

I
don't know
Dorothy

Auntie Em sells crystal out of abandoned
missile silos in Shawnee Co;
gave me my first shot of peach schnapps at 14,
PTSD hits her every Thursday at noon,
tornado siren tests encompassing
Wanamaker Rd in Top-City
usually do the trick

the Wicked Witch of the West really isn't a bad date
weekend homelessness
with Ornette Coleman
chomping out the rhyme of seasons out of
Farmer Love Bones 58 Ford,
hotwired
and another
felony writhing
under my belt, the misconceived
necromancer of the plains
will adjudicate a wink at me after my
veins collapse and the needle
flat lines on the dash

I
don't know
Dorothy

a standard answer
dissented
to a repetitive question
unevenly yoked to any poet
from Kansas

and the wizard keeps on laughing

hollow swallow

it's a hollow swallow

he wants to do the cha-cha with a school
      of dolphins in the Gulf of Mexico

he wants to be a C-Note so he can serenade Laura Flynn
      Boyle at the academy awards

he wants to be a Hollywood mobster so he can have a
      dark skinned suit and a Las Vegas Palace among
      the neon clouds

he wants to slam a six pack of Jack Kerouac and breathe
      to the sounds of a sitcom laugh track

it's a hollow swallow

the hangover of Topeka only lasts
until the bottle is empty downtown

among
>   the gymnastics of freshly
>   pined skateboarders,

among
>   the mechanical chants of
>   WALK-DON'T WALK sermons,

among
>   the withering green islands of
>   concrete ships with Old Glory Masts,

among
>   the rhythm of the white shoed
>   nooners burning calories as well as time,

among
>   the focal points from
>   pencil drawings of architectural youth,

among
>   the Ichabods magnetized by
>   bus schedules-taxi cabs-trolley tours,

among
>   the ATM addicts,
>   the obese trash cans,
>   the comatose Canadian coins lounging in
>   dehydrated fountains at Capital Federal,

there is
>   conformity

there is
        routine

there is Kansas Avenue, there is
Kansas Avenue, there
is Kansas
Avenue

click clack paddy whack the Baron
needs a home

street ghosts...street fog...street calligraphy...

a mutton chopped man with bristled phrases tosses out
monotone metaphors to his 11 year old daughter
in an effort to describe the operatic chants of steam
that creep out of the sewers on West 39th. *Sweetie,
they are...*

street delusions...street mantras...street sermons...

Baron Von Ryborg crosses
39th and Stateline
his fever is at 101

two twenty-year-old sorority sisters are lobbing
scuffed billiards behind the caked windows of Jimmy
Jigger. The cute brunette with
a T-Shirt that promulgates
*If I wanted your opinion
I'd put Flat Dou Jets in your mouth*
slams her fifth shot of Jameson
then she calls out her pool shot

To Jesus and His dead horses

street planes...street manes...street horses...

Eleven years old
what grade is that?
5th?
6th?
Her father guides their translucent
waltz as they follow the Baron into
Prospero's Books
The Sunshine Destroyers
the featured band for Jesus and
His dead horses this evening

45 minutes late
Aussie Pinot Noir and Lorazepam
pirouetting in his veins

the Baron's fever is at 101

    street customs...street fevers...street grins...

the band rambles about 50 foot
women and three
dollar smiles. Von Ryborg's
fever
is at
101

    street lust...street metronome...street melodies

the band is beckoned for an encore, liquid
courage is a street urchin's reciprocated breath
a chorus line lingering within the
REM cycles
of West 39th street

    street demons…street terrors…street dreams

Baron Von Ryborg slams a handful of Lorazepam
and whispers a denunciation
for the street messiahs of the West 39th

To Jesus and His dead horses

    street messiahs…street preachers…street poets

the operatic chants of steam
continue along 39th street
Baron Von Ryborg's fever is at 101
but it is
breaking

the engagement

when you enrapture
a whisper
or an evolving memory
time becomes your
next of kin

pirouetting
among the synapses of thought
continuance lashes out
a mirrored metronome
out of tune

looking for
a riot to hold onto
I now have seasons that
God may not
forgive

my vice and virtue
a cracked window pane affianced
sin and grace
a betrothed progenitor
whose unending argument
lodges logic in an illogical
sacrament

how fragrant,
eventually

(eventually)

present day

cerulean skies conscribe
drifting contingencies, a monotone
chant across vacant midtown
rooftops along West 39th
this evening

she whispered nothing is
the result of immediacy

a five and dime receipt ensnared
on the counter, last week's coffee
stain cracked the linoleum

she whispered nothing is the result
of immediacy

second hand on the clock radio
enters a coma, madness is an
tailor made overcoat in your veins

she
whispered nothing is
the result
of immediacy

cerulean skies conscribe
drifting contingencies, a monotone
chant across vacant midtown
rooftops along West 39th
this evening

and her biological clock
keeps on ticking...

entry number nineteen
-for Kate

 ....and then I pandered her
to bequeath some
spare change
while she was standing at
39th and Broadway
my visions
leaking out
of the wounds
in my arms

she couldn't
spare
a dime

generally
when the sun sets,
one would expect that the
hopes and
dreams of others
would follow the same strands of
light that cascade along the horizon

my thoughts
ramble in their
own tone and slumber
in their
own timeline

Reincarnated visions...
the human condition in
lyrical form...

Gate, Gate, Paragate, Parasamgate, Bodhi Svaha

the brew of silence...
thoughts
of a friend

Revenge isn't a dish
best served cold...
It's foremost intent is to be served
frozen and donated on a hot day
sunlight slowly melts the ice of forgotten time
what appears refreshing and calm
lingers among that which is evaporated by forgiveness
what melts into the abyss of chaos isn't
what was beaten down

It's what her smile takes away

when I pandered for that smile,
she rewarded me with love.
battle scars soothed in silence
thoughts
of a friend

her thursdays

…and it was one of those late nights
when the echoes of sleep ring in your
ears and the memories of restlessness
tumble in your heart

I can't remember the last
dream that I had that was encased
in color. The dialogue
is always fragmented in mine.

love, if unblemished is eternal

the phrase has stuck in my
head for three weeks; the mysteries of
REM cycles.

I don't smoke but this
cigarette is keeping me
entertained. The ashes
red with envy
jealous that they will
never be green

virginal

I've burned three Camels so far

A cow is bellowing at two
a.m. It's a welcomed sound.

Bovine solos are unheard
at 39th and Main.

I remember when
falling in love was
a chore. The process
has been coming with
relative ease but
it's become

fragmented,
sub consequential,
shadowed,

I miss you…Jameson…bring me…the blue…ribbon

her voice
cracked and
solitary
her hair
auburn with a
twist
of
verboten
lust

I've run out of matches
but I have three more cigarettes to burn

for her
today is
a Thurdsay

the winter of my discontent
-for Tiffany

reverberated echoes and recycled candlewicks

no response

unsealed envelopes and an empty matchbox

no response

a scrap of paper laments
inside Union Station after it
seceded from of her purse

> *In many ways, your wanderlust has*
> *continued since you met me.*
> *What grinds us together*
> *tears us apart.*
> *Winter has set in and in many*
> *ways we have let our own*
> *fires become winterized.*
> *A time of rekindling*
> *Spring cannot exist without winter's*
> *perseverance.*
> *The dawn of our lives is very close . . .*
> *I love you.*

painted ceilings and unplowed driveways

no response

three bums argue over tin cans outside of a Starbucks,
a cat creeps into a vagabond's alley

no response

whenever I dial her
phone number,
there is repose,
but there is
no response

after I Jackson Pollocked myself
over a young woman's heart,
and redecorated an unmarked grave,
I realized that not all
continents are landlocked
during the freedom of the
winter
of my
discontent

The Five Breaths

I'm a fool who acts like a genius,
who acts like a fool
to give the impression
that I am a genius who acts like a fool.
It's so genius,
It fools me sometimes.

- The Weltanschauung
of Bipolar Steve

I. Puraka

The sobriety riots continue
inside a rusted Maytag at
the Lovely Bubbly on east 69th.

I forgot to empty the front pockets of
my Levi's again.

Sweating like a bumblebee
with honey for rent,
rehab has cauterized my mood.

The plateletpheresis of 25 grams of
OxyContin
deliquesce from my blood stained
trousers;

a transmogrification of bargain
basement group therapy.

I hum *Holiday in Cambodia* as the

revolutions continue
pondering how many pills will
survive the supernova of memory.

Hers or mine?

The antecessor of each bloodstain
hides in the mire of detox;
yet screams bequeathed to their own
name are never heard.

Rinse, Recycle, Repeat.

The sobriety riots continue,
no treaty in sight.

II. Abhyantara Kumbhaka

The string less marionettes of self-rape:

Unconditional love
kneads the air
a white striated fog
threading the shadows.

III. Diffusion

Satori
along
the roadside –
A crushed
turtle

IV. Rechaka

… and the pendulum keeps on
swinging.

As benevolence evolves, uncontested
karma reciprocates.

It's a surgical carving of your soul.

Not a repairable tear
Or
An erosion of causation –

It's a deliberate
Corroding
Exsanguination.

(salud)

In retaliation,
the evaluation of your heart is not
based
on the typography of your scars
but in your mockery of each swipe
from the blade.

…and the pendulum keeps on
swinging.

V. Bahya Kumbhaka

The sobriety riots continue
inside a rusted Maytag at
the Lovely Bubbly on east 69th.

I forgot to empty the front pockets of
my Levi's again.

Sweating like a bumblebee
with honey for rent,
rehab has cauterized my mood.
The plateletpheresis of her obituary
deliquesce from my blood stained
trousers;
A transmogrification of bargain
basement group therapy.

I hum *Holiday in Cambodia* as the
revolutions continue
pondering how many of her
handwritten poems will
survive the supernova of memory.

Hers or mine?

The antecessor of each bloodstain
hides in the mire of detox;
yet screams bequeathed to their own
name are never heard.

Rinse, Recycle, Repeat.

The sobriety riots continue,
no treaty in sight.

an open letter to Lew Welch written by
an answer to a question no one asked

dear Lew,

if you see
Kurt Cobain,
you tell that son of a bitch that
he owes me $40

in 2016
I purchased tickets
to go see the
*Bowie-Prince-Ali-Gene Wilder-Merle Haggard-Glenn
Fry-Paul Katner-Harper Lee-Morley Shafer-Gary
Shandling-Alan Rickman-Leonard Cohen and Abe Vigoda*
reunion tour

and none of them showed

and tell Kurt
that in 2016
Nevermind turned
twenty five
and we are still
chasing dollar bills
on fishing hooks
with our Anthony Weiners out

Lew,
on
August 13, 2016
Jayden Ugwuh
and
Montell Ross
were gunned down,
died in each
others arms
and
hashtag toddlers lives matter
never had
an obligatory march
or an obsequious riot
in Kansas City

Lew,
when I was twenty,
 I met a doe eyed stripper with
chronic gingivitis at Baby Dolls *(what the hell
was her name, eh, we will call her
Cherry Sherry)*
I asked Cherry Sherry if she earned fat
stacks or made mad cheddar or
whatever the hell kids say these days
and Cherry Sherry said
well
the pay sucks but I get all the greasy
chicken fried steak that I want when I work
on Friday nights during NASCAR weekend

and I said *really* and
she said
yeah

Lew,
I asked Cherry Sherry if she enjoys the career choice
recommendation that her high school counselor
bequeathed to her after she decided to skip third period

French and meet Steve *Two Smokes* McGee in a '58
Studebaker that was stalled behind the
Kum and Go for a therapy session with quart of
moonshine while mainlining self-acceptance
and Cherry Sherry said
well
the pay sucks but I get all the greasy
chicken fried steak that I want when I work
on Friday nights during NASCAR weekend
and I said *really* and
she said
yeah

cherry sherry said
well I gotta go
there is a group of MFA poets
who just returned from AWP sitting back
there in corner, rocking out to old Devo cover bands
and THEY usually PAY pretty well

and Lew,
when I asked Cherry Sherry how much she usually makes
during greasy chicken fried steak and NASCASR nights
which are on Fridays at Baby Dolls
she replied

a hundred and eighty three dollars and sixty four cents

and I said *really* and
she said

(yeah)

on the table,
I tossed a 50 cent coupon for Shake and Bake that
expired during the Clinton Administration,
my only copy of
The Outlaw Bible of American Poetry,
and my regurgitation of Maslow's
Hierarchy of Needs

Cherry Sherry
had my baby
but
I haven't
seen
her
since

sincerely,

an answer to a question no one asked

an open letter from three plenty of fishes

Dear Swipe Right,

Why do you always wear a
hat? Are all of your profile pics
current? Do you have a recent
pic? You look nothing
like your profile pic. You
look better than your profile
pic. Can I see what you look like
right now?

I only date men who are
taller than me. I only date
African Americans. I only date
Latinos. I don't a date outside
of my race. I don't date African
Americans. I don't date Latinos. I
only date men shorter than
me. I believe in monogamy. I'm
only interested in open relationships.
I don't date men at all.

You don't smoke. I'm 420 friendly. I
don't do drugs. I'm a social drinker. I
drink wine. I only drink beer. I inhale
cigar smoke. I won't drink in public. I
abstain from alcohol.

I won't sleep with you on a
first date. I will only meet you for coffee
when I see you. I won't go to your
place for a first date. I'll cook you dinner at
my place the first time I wink at you. Let's
Netflix and chill. I don't own a TV or have the internet.
Do you have any mint flavored condoms?

I'm blocking you. I just sent you
a wink. I poked you. Sent you a
smile. I sent you my makes or breaks.
I answered your essay questions. I added you to
my favorites. I'm blocked you again.

Let's exchange numbers. I don't give
my number out until after the first date.
I'll friend you on Facebook. Follow you on
Instagram. I'll retweet you. I'll say hello to
you. Leave me alone but I still want you to marry me.

Sincerely,

Swipe Left

preface

when your entertainment comes in a can
and you realize that your can opener is broken,
and your dog ate your church key because your resume
    was stale,
and you realize that the vaginas that haunt you in your
    dreams are nothing more than discontinued lean
    cuisine casseroles that you have burnt in your
    microwave while you mulled over your third
    eviction notice
and you are too tired
too drunk
too crunked
too oversexed
too under sexed
too lack of free sex
too sodium free
too fat free
too gluten free
too GMO free
too condoms free for college freshman
too sleazy
too sleepy
too dopey
too grumpy
too anti-Trumpy
too care

and you watch infinite digital dialogues transverse your
>social media status update and no one really
contemplates the lighthouse in your mind among
the tsunami of insanity
and you watch the ebb and tide of twitter feeds,
Instagram likes, snap chat face swaps and you
have purged these recycled conversations
without comment
and you watch food bank lines en mass despair, plasma
centers donate lifelines to
the forgotten dreams of childhood that hashtag
fightforfifteen merely drowns
and you watch suicide/depression ward lobbies weep and
moan during the ethereal silence of man
and you watch the unrehearsed screams of poverty
and you watch
and you watch
and you watch
so no
no
I don't
watch
reality
TV.

murphy's law

Drakkar Noir
air fresheners,
even
Gonish
cones
4 for a dollar
will not
dissipate
the scent
of an
ex.

self help

the idea

coagulates

inside
of my
head

I need
to
learn
to
melt

searching for a voice

miles davis and I
went out lookin' for ms right
the other night

i
remember
my first time

dana scully showed up
pinned me
to my overused easy boy recliner
impaled me
with that midsummer horizon stare of hers
she whispered
semantic symbolism
semantic symbolism
'till I passed out

and when I opened my eyes
 i saw a young girl
who slit her wrists
and a poet
dripped
onto
the
floor

i wanted to have her pale palms read
by those who knew her, but they replied
not all pencils have erasers

miles davis gargled
his hypodermic voice
then replied

string less guitars
    overfed dresser drawers
    pigeon shit on discarded pages of
    the Wall Street journal.
    reversed circumcisions,
    road rage,
    frightened coins in a dry urinal.

strap me to your water logged crucifix
    pitch me over that bridge you burned long ago
    I am underneath the water's edge like
    prechewed gum after a seven o'clock show

i said
do wop be bop
and who the fuck
is miles davis anyway?

i guess I just
wanted
to make him
proud
of
  . . .

the acoustical resonance when doves cry

(I)

pomp and circumstance
among the reverberated IV
lines, her last drop of
Cytarabine hibernates
on the marrow in
the marrow of life

(II)

ink dehydrates on
an inaugural lease as
the open road of residency pacifies
the angst of homelessness among
a choir of rental keys

(III)

maternity ward, 3:05 am
first born swaddling in
syncopated hues of sleep, first
steps into fatherhood syndicate
the soliloquy of silence

until the last tie is broken
-for Linzi

she scans the ceilings
in my apartment
for the faces of history
neither one of us
have ever endured

a fifth grade English teacher collecting eraser shavings
    underneath the desks of endless students
      in memorandum for the poems that are washed
      away during the mentorship of life
a homeless family asleep in the pews of Union Station
    an injunction to centuries of aqueous dreams
    that leaned on the rusted rails in endless
    railyards…in tune with the evicerated tears of
    hope
a lost love lounging within the spirals of one's own skin
    immortalized in the object permanence of youth

Malbec stains on the floor, Miles Davis
lamenting an alternative
take of
Kind of Blue
on the stereo

sleeping in the shadows of
the laughter within the lingering
stars, she buries her smiles
within the blood poems

she exhumes, droplets of verse
flickering within the idolatries of
her own
inexperience
until the last
tie is broken
she whispers

until
the last
tie
is
broken

the biography of Christian O'Keeffe

enshrined among
cherub chants of morose
calligraphy
irises made of moth wings
were the sextons
in the cemeteries
of his scars

a lost echo lingers

a shadowed
afterthought
besieged in his verses for
your enlightenment

* *Irises Made of Moth Wings* by Christian O'Keeffe (Crisis Chronicles Press, 2014)

Rides In

Visibly on treatment
Disguised in mind
After an unattached master nominates love
Addiction...is love

vacant sons and entombed monotones
candlesticks mimic belligerent
booze hounds, we are
stripped to the bear
moans
I'll charge the ride then let
you stay

drunken nights in fogged catharsis
hippie mambas with broken wrists, she'll
take my chance with death's kiss, pulled
her rubes out
yesterday

I know
where to fake it
my conflicted patience
it's my name branded on her mind among
fields of cotton candy suicides and ...

Visibly on treatment
Disguised in mind
After an unattached master nominates love
Rehab...is love

make a plea then wreak myself, disoriented
nights in film noir motels
my better half is not for sale

I'll solicit Gestaltian
lines and
then
I'll wait

vicodin and maybe I'll numb a song
trazodone then maybe sleep will sing along
transubstantiation is
even on my mind
seek until noon,
my solicited sacrament of
staying
alive

Visibly on treatment
Disguised in mind
After an unattached master nominates love
Love
Is

...

A side-effect of the military industrial complex, Jameson Bayles was born at a hospital at Forbes Field AFB just south of Topeka, KS. By the age of eighteen, Jameson had participated in a refueling mission with F-16s over the skies in South Dakota, stood atop an active missile silo, and was the bait in a counter-terrorism exercise with Air Force Special Forces at Whiteman AFB. After watching Krist Novoselic obtain a head injury at the 1992 MTV Music Awards, Jameson decided to pursue the path of becoming a poet. In addition to being a roving correspondent for Poetrybay, Jameson co-curated the 2016 KC Poetry Throwdown with Jason Ryberg at Prospero's Books in Kansas City, MO. Having been published in numerous literary journals and magazines, Jameson resides in Kansas City, Missouri and can be reached at jamesonbayles @gmail.com.

The cover photos for this series were contributed by Jon Bidwell, a photographer who lives and works in Kansas. To view more of his work, visit him at www.instagram.com/jonbidwell.

This project was made possible, in part, by generous support from the Osage Arts Community.

Osage Arts Community provides temporary time, space and support for the creation of new artistic works in a retreat format, serving creative people of all kinds — visual artists, composers, poets, fiction and nonfiction writers. Located on a 152-acre farm in an isolated rural mountainside setting in Central Missouri and bordered by ¾ of a mile of the Gasconade River, OAC provides residencies to those working alone, as well as welcoming collaborative teams, offering living space and workspace in a country environment to emerging and mid-career artists. For more information, visit them at osageac.org

Dedicated to Dorie Renee Hogan

(1974-1996)

www.ingramcontent.com/pod-product-compliance
Lightning Source LLC
Chambersburg PA
CBHW021451080526
44588CB00009B/794